Alphabets Learning

by

Smooth Vibes

ISBN: 9798644450756

DEDICATION

Dedicated to all Dyslexic kids for their courage to learn.

<u>Guide</u>

Learning through colors

Step 1:

Connect the dots

Step 2:

Fill the void with your favorite colors

Step 3:

C Repeat till the end and enjoy along.

Alphabet learning for Dyslexic Kids

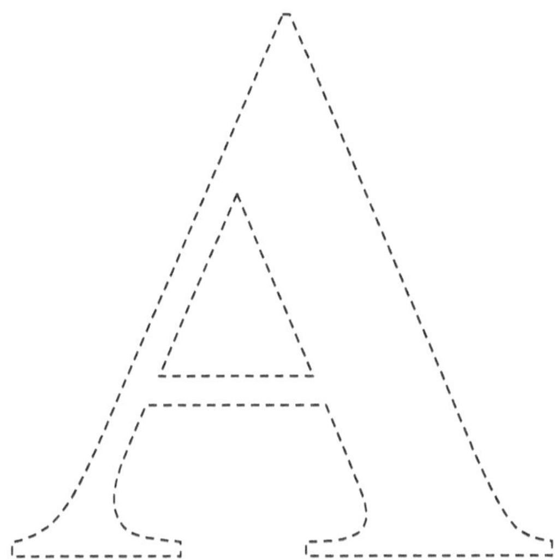

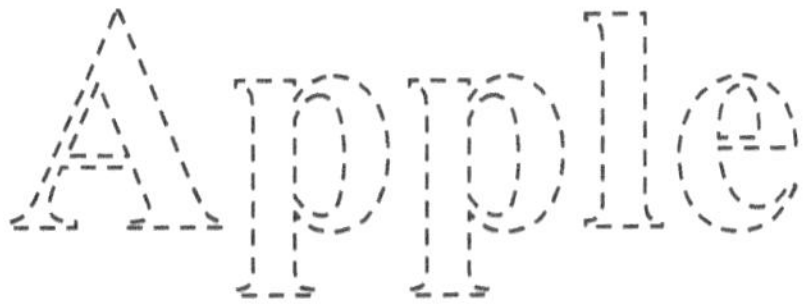

Apple is a fruit.

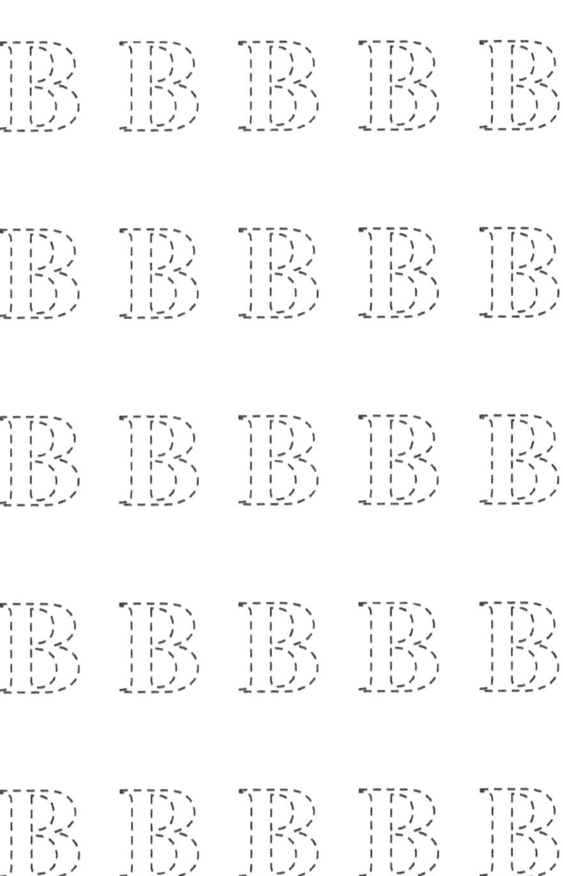

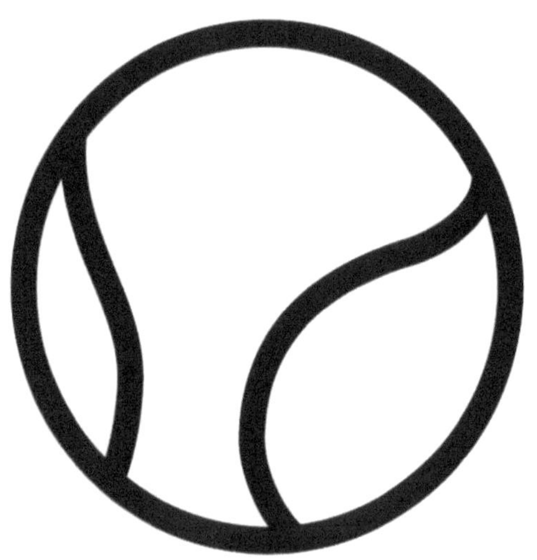

Ball is a playing object.

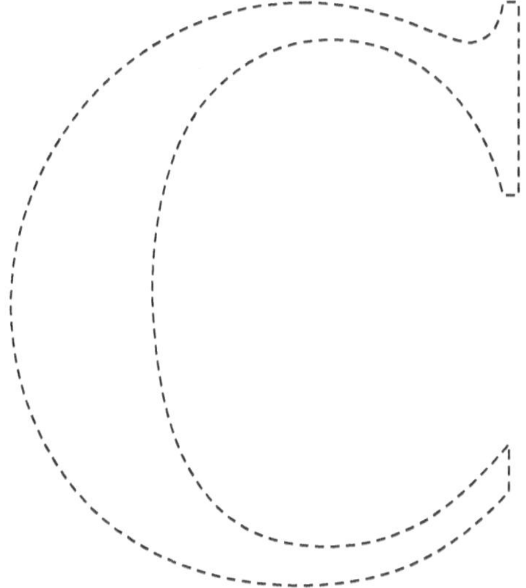

Cat is an animal.

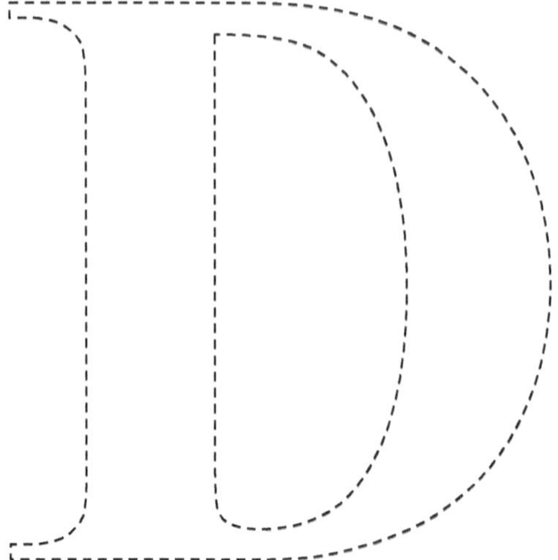

D

D D D D D

D D D D D

D D D D D

D D D D D

D D D D D

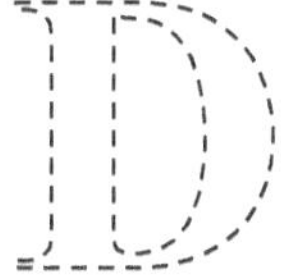

Dog is an animal.

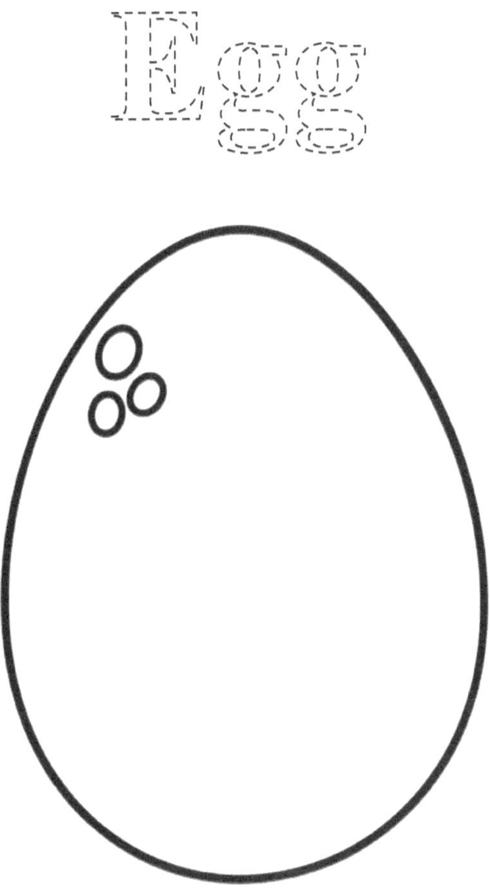

Egg is an Egg ☺

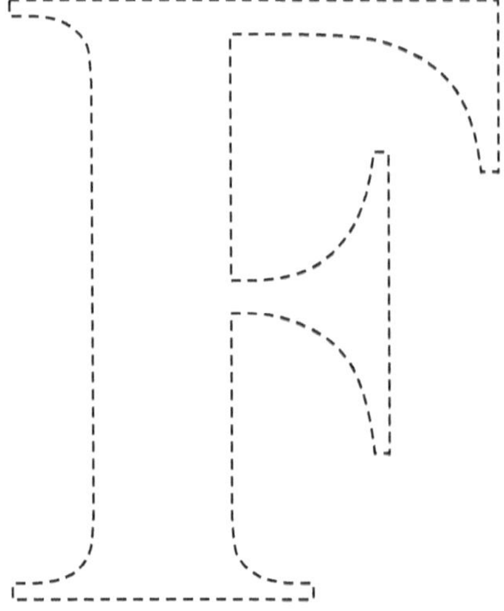

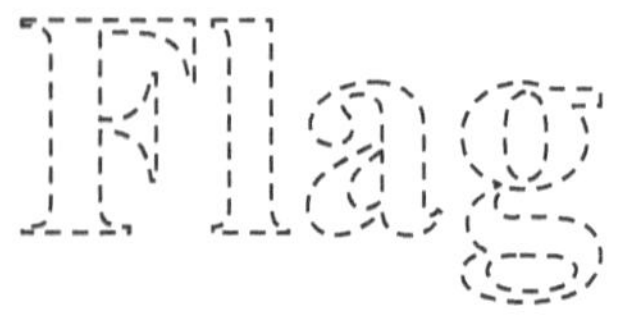

Flag is a piece of cloth, used as the symbol or emblem of a country.

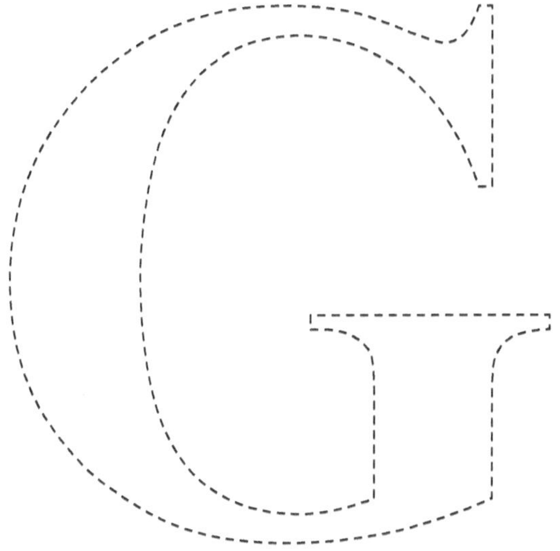

Gift is a present.

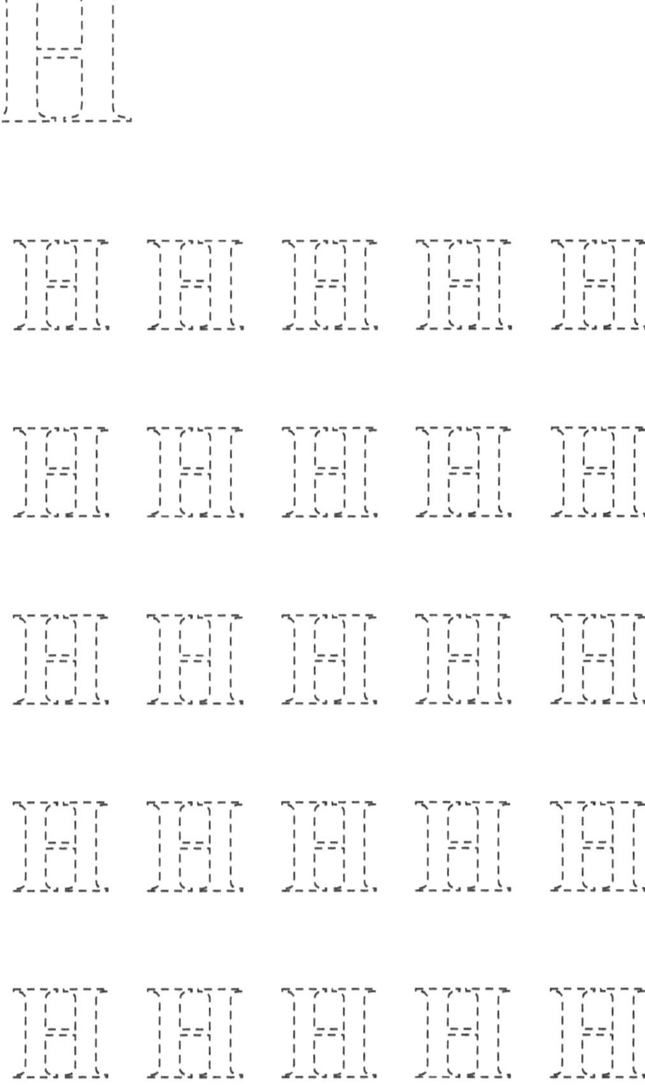

House

House is where you live.

27

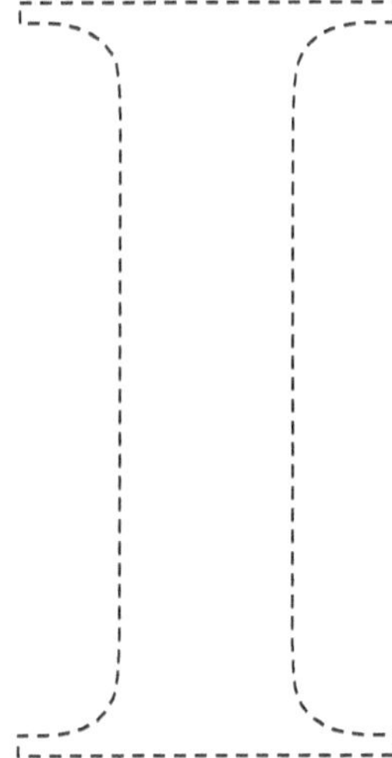

Ice Cream

Ice cream is a soft, sweet frozen food.

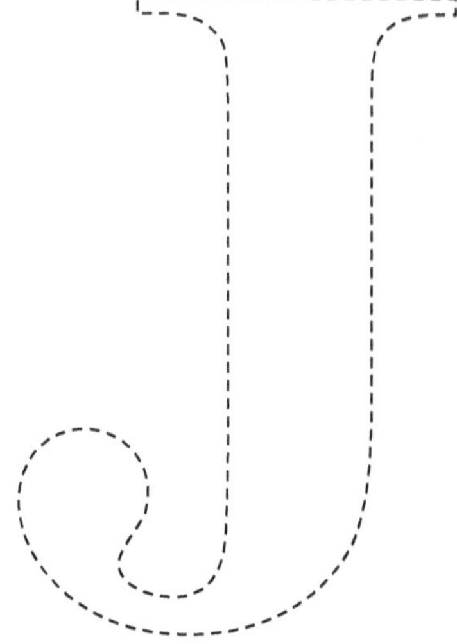

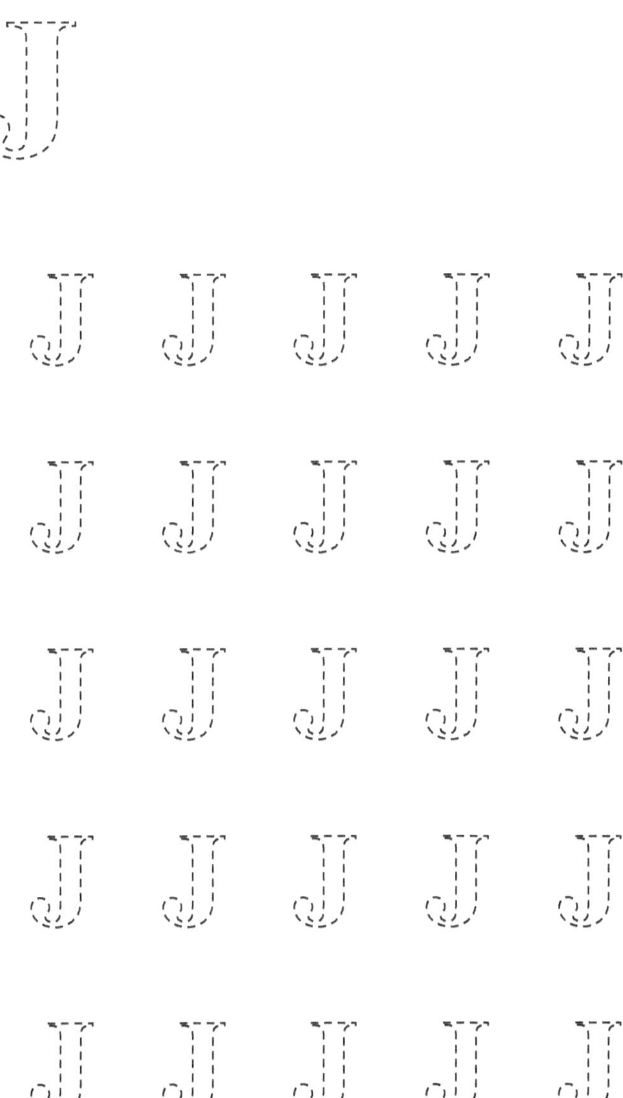

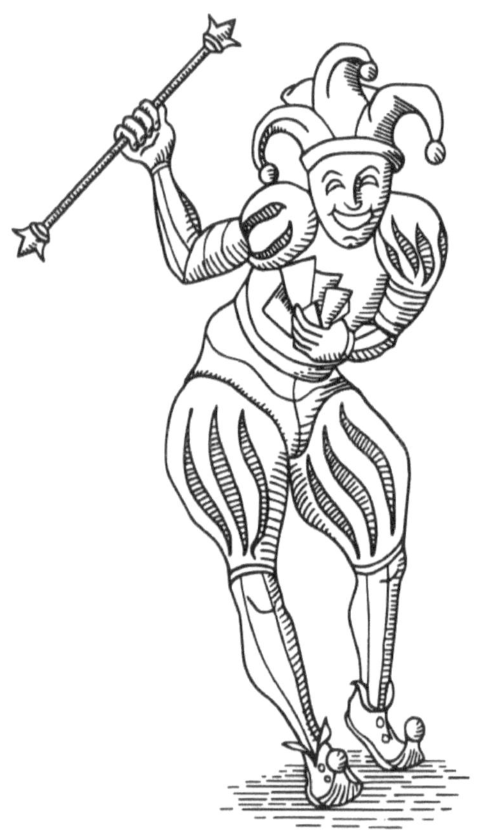

Joker is a comedian.

K

K K K K K

K K K K K

K K K K K

K K K K K

K K K K K

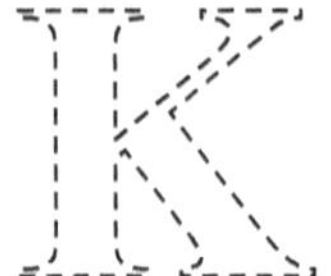

Kite

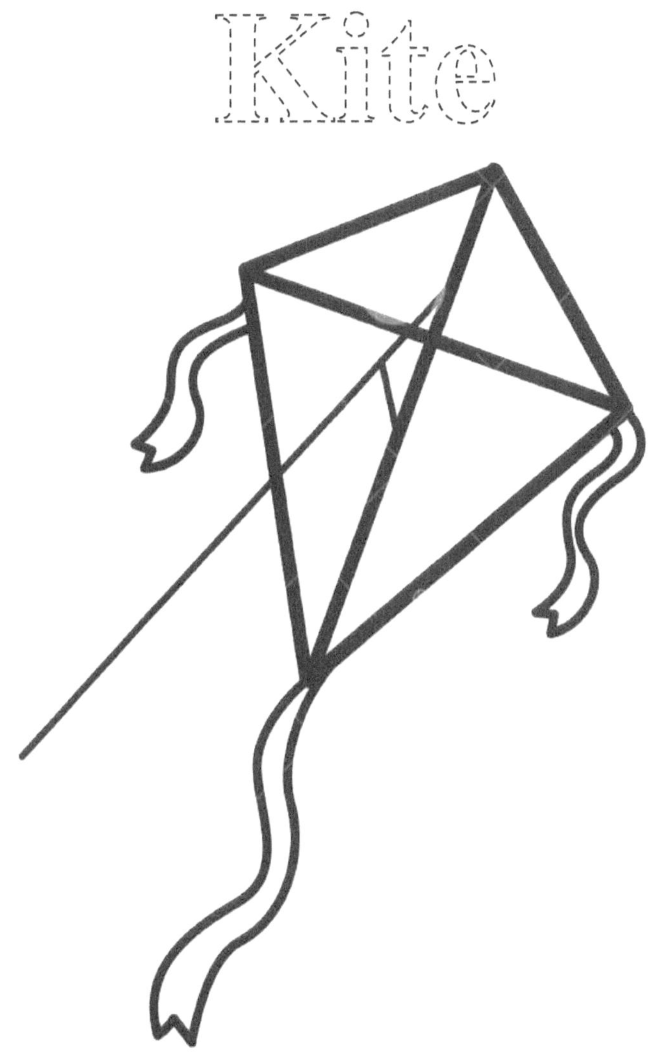

Kite is a toy flown in wind.

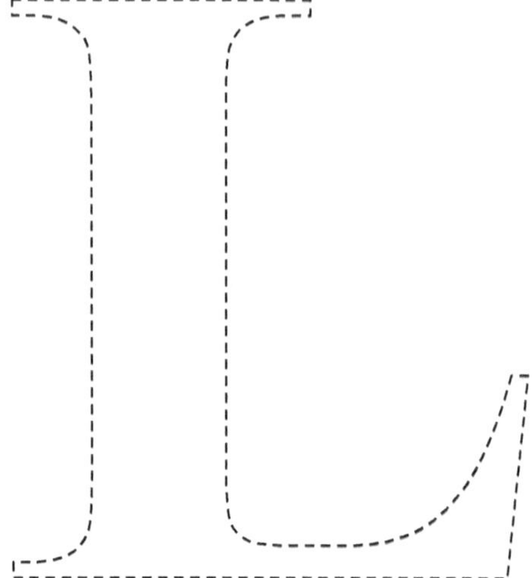

L

L L L L L

L L L L L

L L L L L

L L L L L

L L L L L

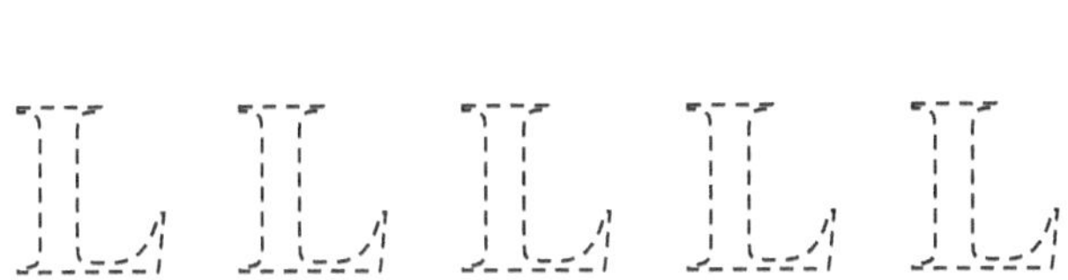

Leaves are the organs of photosynthesis.

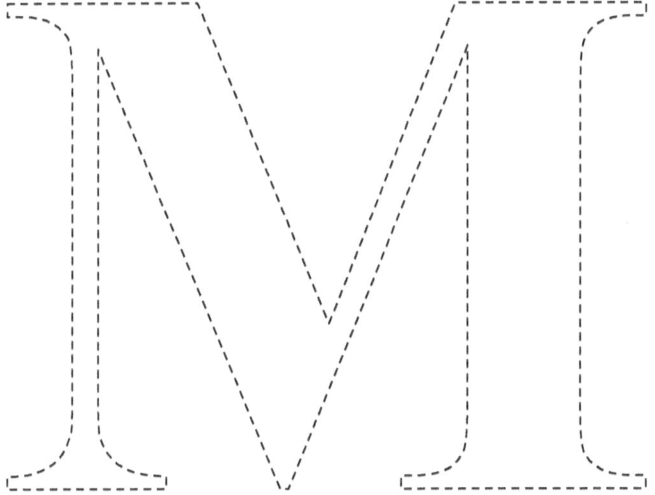

M

M M M M M

M M M M M

M M M M M

M M M M M

M M M M M

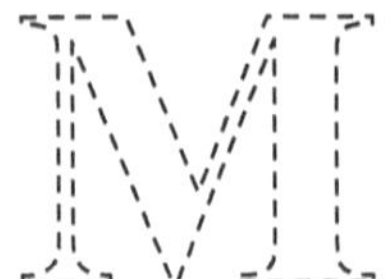

Moon is the natural satellite.

42

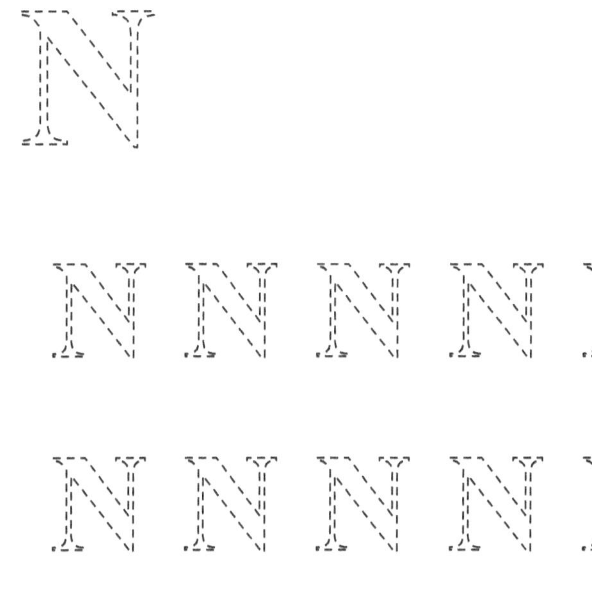

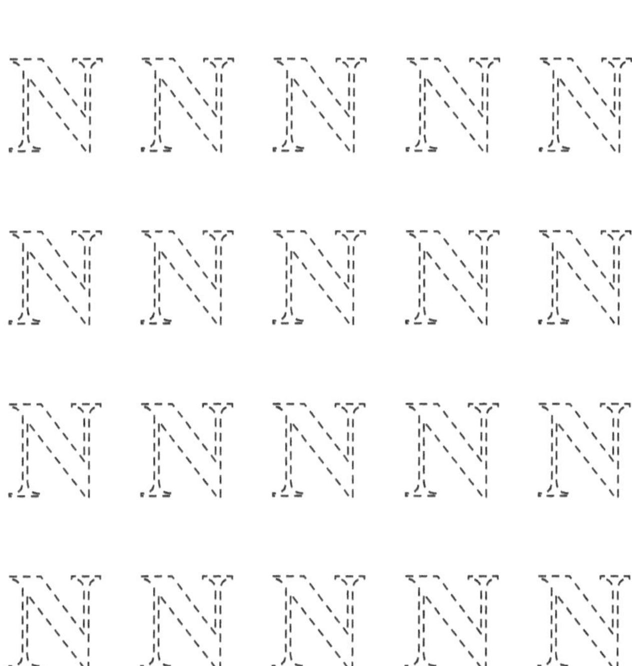

Nest

A structure or place made or chosen by a bird for laying eggs.

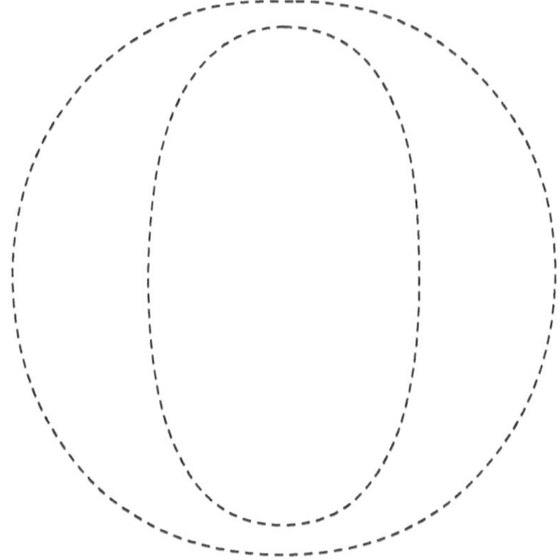

An owl is a bird.

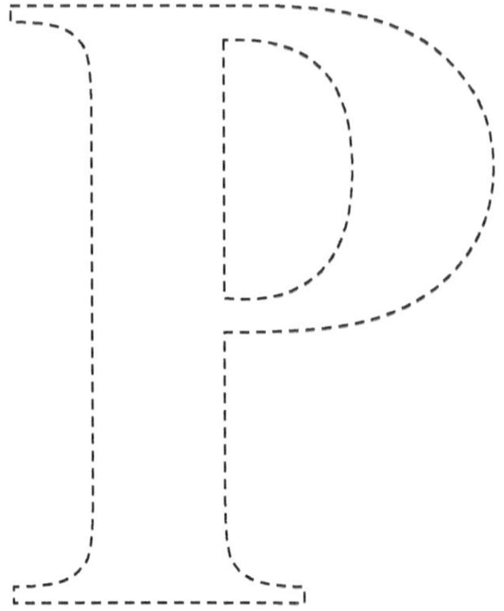

P

P P P P P

P P P P P

P P P P P

P P P P P

P P P P P

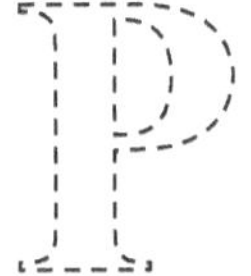

Piano is a musical instrument.

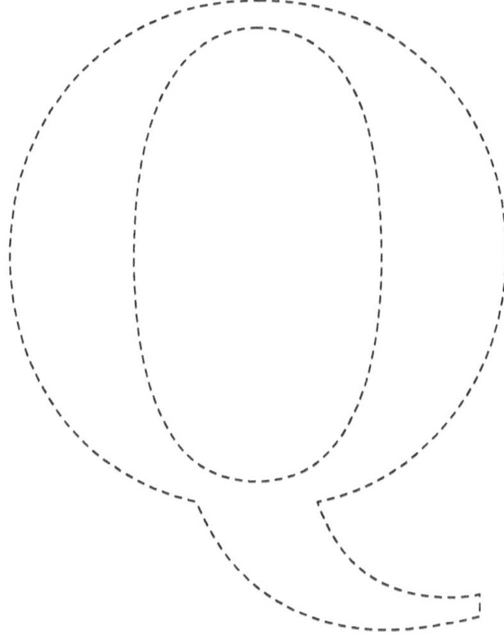

Queen

Queen is a female ruler of an independent state.

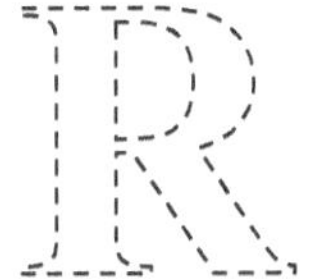

Rose is a flower.

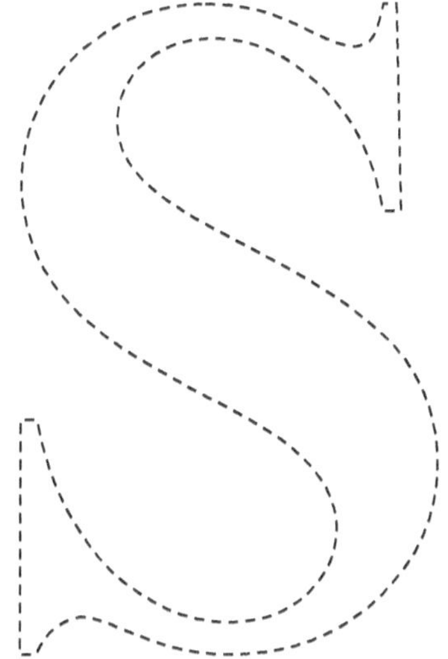

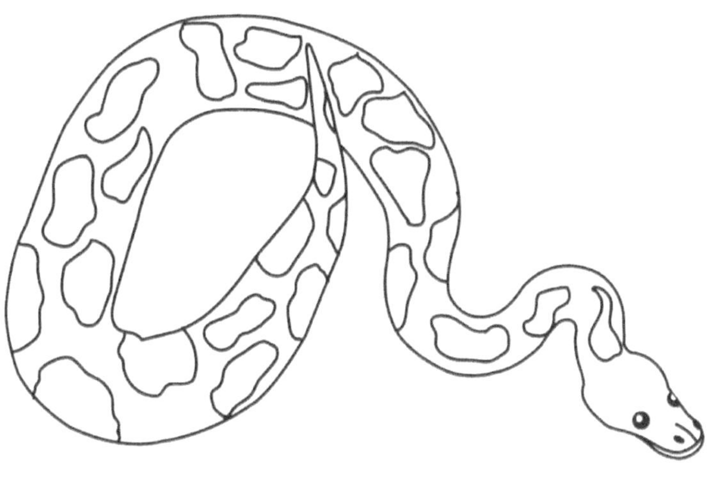

Snake is a long limbless reptile.

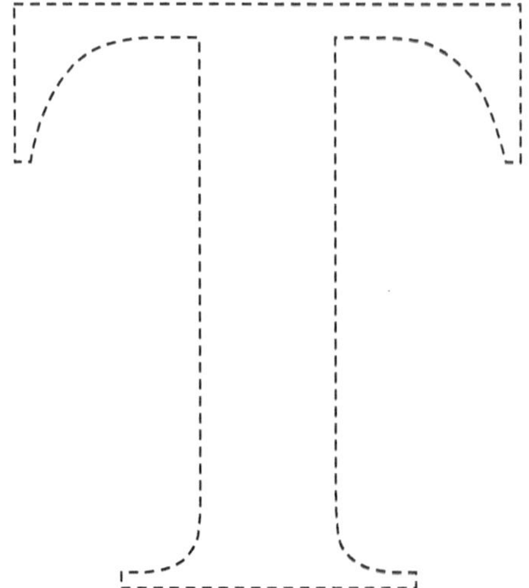

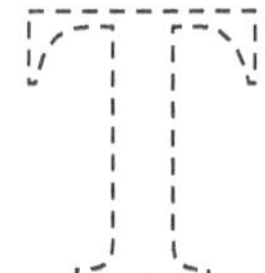

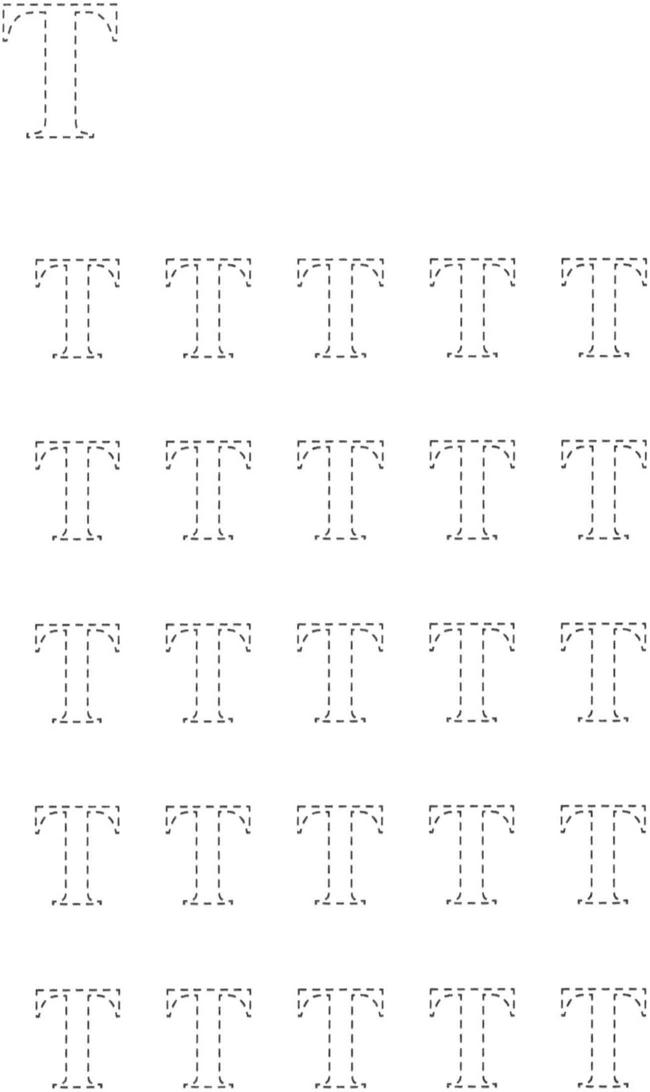

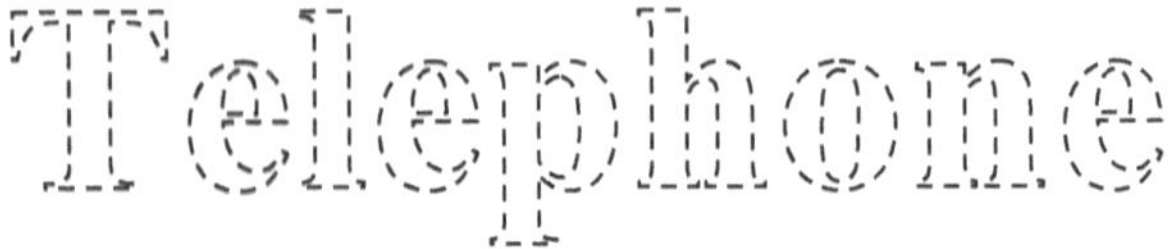

Telephone is a communication device.

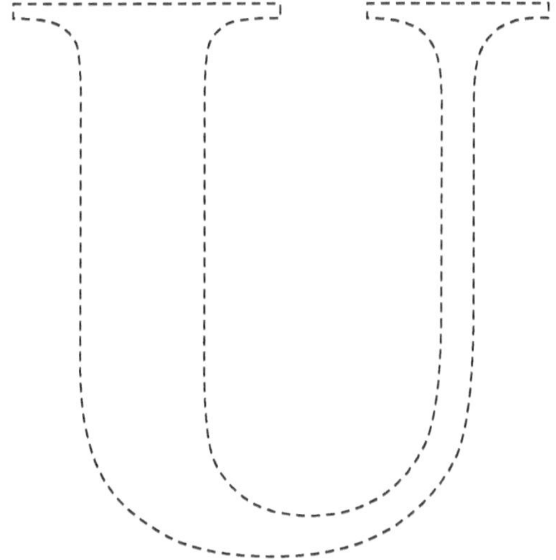

Umbrella is a circular canopy of cloth, used as protection against rain.

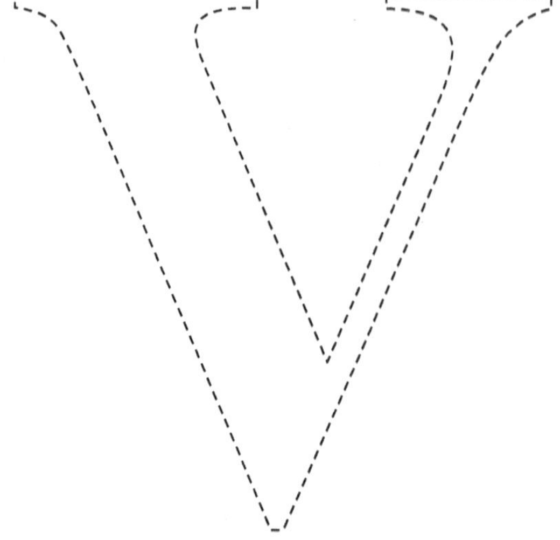

Violin is a musical instrument.

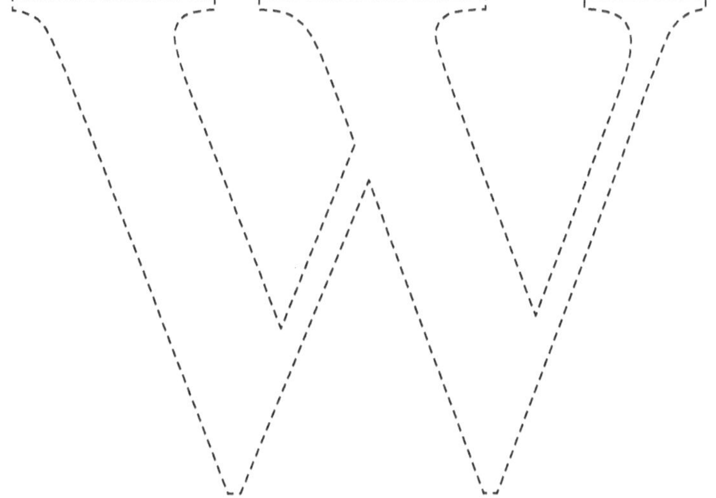

Watch

Watch is a small timepiece worn on one's wrist.

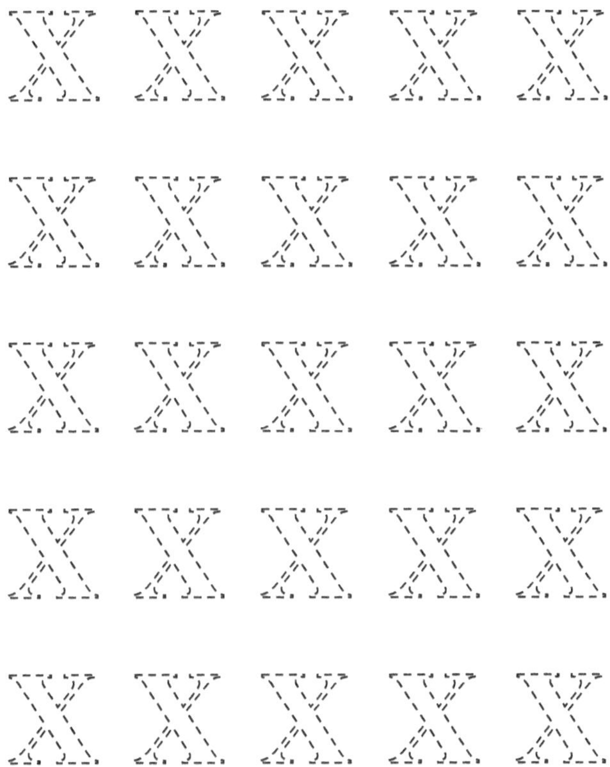

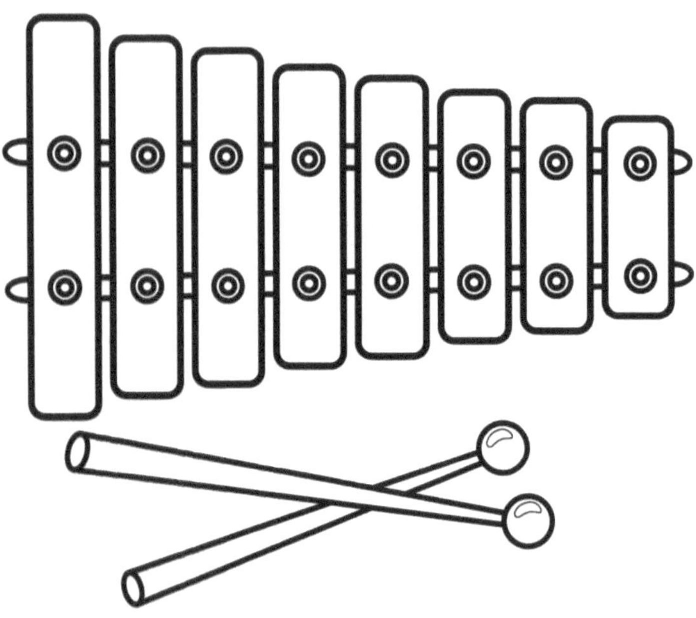

Xylophone is a musical instrument played by striking a row of wooden bars.

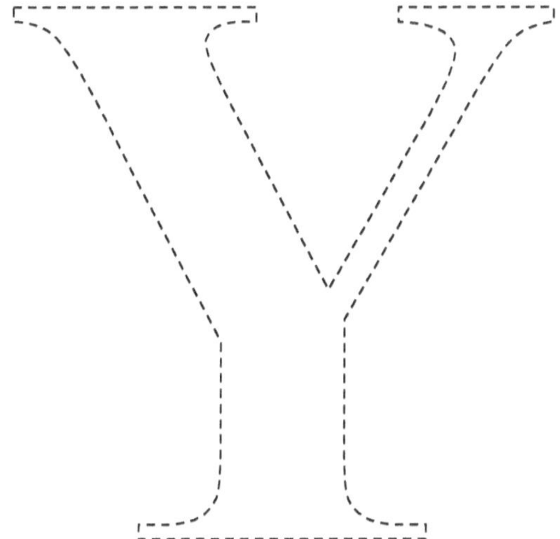

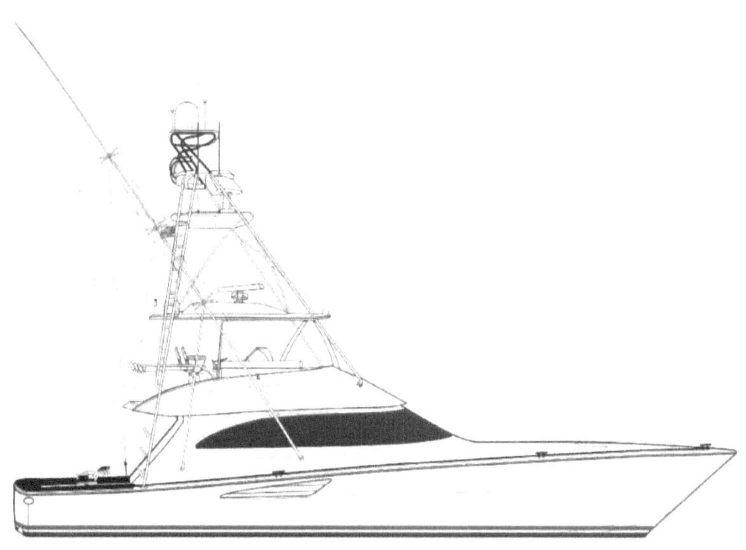

Yacht is a medium-sized sailing boat.

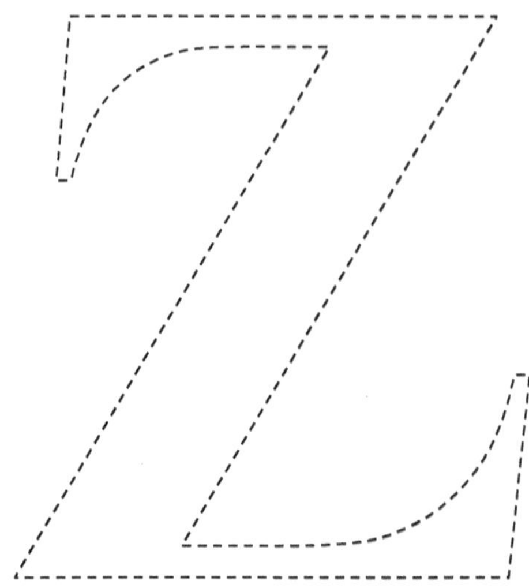

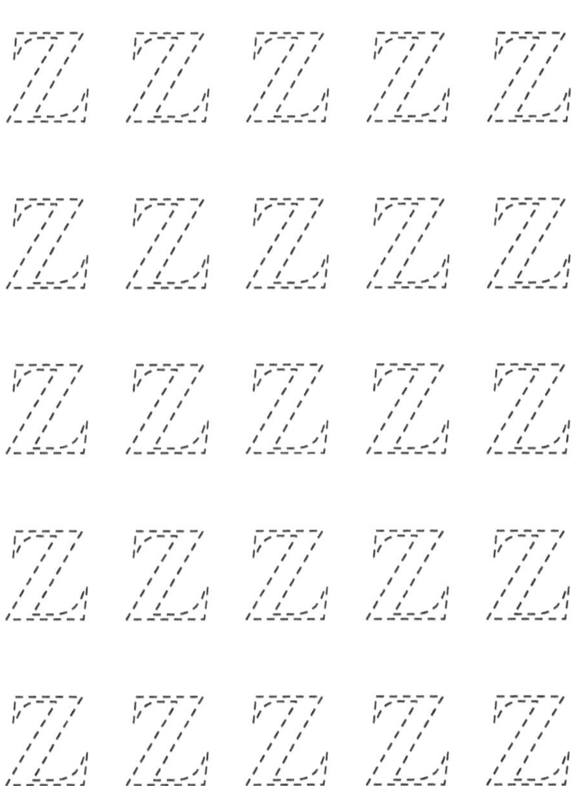

Zoo is an establishment, which maintains a collection of wild animals.